reel LIFE

Tommy DeJosia

Reel Life

Tommy DeJosia

Silenced Press

Reel Life. Copyright © 2009 by Silenced Press. All rights reserved. Printed in the United States of America- Columbus, Ohio. No part of this book may be used or reproduced in any manner whatsoever without written permission except in the case of brief quotations embodied in critical articles and reviews.

First Printing. First Edition.

ISBN-13: 978-0-9792410-1-7
ISBN-10: 0-9792410-1-4

Library of Congress Control Number: †

More information available at:

www.silencedpress.com

SCENES:

EXT. BOAT – NIGHT [8]
INT. BROOKLYN APARTMENT – DAWN [9]
EXT. BAR – NIGHT [10]
EXT: BEACH – SUNSET [12]
EXT. BOAT – SUNSET [14]
EXT. FIRE ISLAND - 2 A.M. [16]
INT. CAR – DAY [17]
EXT. HAMPTONS BAR - WAY PAST MIDNIGHT [19]
INT. GUAS' CAR – NIGHT [21]
INT. BANK – DAY [23]
INT. GIRL'S BEDROOM – MIDNIGHT [24]
INT. SUBURBAN HOME – NIGHT [26]
INT. MIND - DAY/NIGHT [28]
INT. COMPUTER ROOM – NIGHT [30]
INT. BEDROOM – NIGHT [32]
INT. CAR – NIGHT [34]
INT. KITCHEN – NIGHT [35]
INT. JOURNAL – TWILIGHT [37]
INT. MIRROR – NIGHT [38]
EXT. BOAT – EVENING [39]
EXT. DOCK – DAY [41]
INT. LOFT – DUSK [42}

This book has been modified from its original version. It has been formatted to fit this page.

```
                    *
                           *
              *
         *
   * * * * * * *
                                              *
    *
     *                            *
      *                    *
```

EXT. BOAT - NIGHT

Lights
stretched across
sea = shore

        Fire Island

_____

∧∧∧∧∧∧∧∧∧∧∧∧∧
[boat] anchored
∧∧∧∧∧∧∧∧∧∧∧∧∧
∧∧∧∧∧∧∧∧∧∧∧∧∧

b u i **l** d i **n** g s

L   O   N   G   I   S   L
          A   N   D

INT. BROOKLYN APARTMENT - DAWN

Alcohol stains my breath.
I glance out the
bedroom window…

black sky evolving blue mo(u)rning.

There's a sadness
in this room.

It eats at the
solar plexis
of the internal
universe.

TOMMY: (V.O.)
Too much of the same bullshit
keeps me stagnant.

The bags under my eyes
aren't lonely anymore,
they now have the company
of sleep.

EXT. BAR - NIGHT

Silver moon
the threat of showers

non-existent

…

there she stands

&

she calls my name

SHE:
Tommy D!

I turn.

6 million tons of pressure
focused on the center
of the chest

beauty is a result
of perceived
tension

+

F3ar of
R➔(eject) ion

::deep breath::

:
:
:
:
:
:

life is a
sequence of
events
:
:
:
:
:
:
take the chance
=
I speak -----?

EXT: BEACH - SUNSET

a fading sun slides behind

horizon

where have all the gulls gone?

a summer breeze
a seagull sings

a car pulls up

EYE
[i]

step out wearing
a blazer and a tie

::walks to the bay::

…picks up a rock…

::tosses::

r i p p l e s

his thoughts

mis+placed

EXT. BOAT - SUNSET

As a flock of seagulls fly by, my friends and I watch, as the smoke from the dutch expands with the universe and all our problems disintegrate with one long draw of the lung.

::exhale::

The sounds of the gulls' voice sweep across the Great South Bay. No one, and I mean no one could forget a moment like this.

Four kids with no place to go but off the shore on the southern edge of Long Island. We escape reality into a mental dream state.

::inhale::
::exhale::

red
sun
falls
from the
west

questions postulate brain/water [wave]

"tell me, would you rather fly

OR

go back in time?"

EXT. FIRE ISLAND - 2 A.M.

*

                                                                                    *

                 *
                N

        *

                                             *

W   o   E

*
                    *

                               *
                S

        *

             *

...a compass will direct my motives
till the stars shine...

INT. CAR – DAY

Traffic
Traffic
Traffic

sunRISE hwy

BBP

like

the sky
&
the pen

can the ink of this thought
expand with the
uni
verse
?

somanydreams
so little…

well, you know…

too bad time is symmetric

cause she speeds (55mph?)
   through my mind

and all I want is

a reason
2
let
go

...

EXT. HAMPTONS BAR - WAY PAST MIDNIGHT

(female)-- loving every movement she makes…

$$F_g = \frac{Gm_1m_2}{r^2}$$

the force of two bodies
pulls me in closer
as we
tango

in the sky

a hazy
dazy
phased
moon

[cause]
&
effect

Tidal ^^^^^^
^^^^^^^^^^^
^^^^^^^^^^^

gravity simply
made me fall in
7OV3

with the

m(ocean)
ofherhips

INT. GUAS' CAR - NIGHT

Rainstorm
Windshield wipers
Silent voices
"Explosions in the sky"
Street lights
Reflection off road
Red lights
Left turns
Hospital road
Sunrise highway
Blinkers
Nicholls road

GUAS:
Maybe we've been chilling too much.

I nod.

TOMMY:
Yeah man. I should be creating more.

Guas nods
the beard on his face
grows with the seconds

Church street

Stop sign
Home

TOMMY:
Call me tomorrow.

GUAS:
No doubt man.

I exit car

INT. BANK - DAY

$$$$ → invested → in her eyez → my life →
left b+hind…

my <3
is like an empty
bank account

looking for a loan
to fill the void

I sleep
not to dream
but
to find
my only
way
out of the
sadness
that
keepz
men

$!73NT

INT. GIRL'S BEDROOM - MIDNIGHT

{She}ets cover
my naked
body

her
hand

care
ss
es
'

my back

GIRL:
Cuddle with me.

TOMMY: (V.O.)
Why the fuck am I here?

She kisses my forehead.

TOMMY:
I have to go.

I jump out of bed

wearing only socks…

I grab my
under
wear

,

pants

,

& shirt

and bolt out the door…
she
s c r e a m s

GIRL:
Am I gonna see you again?

INT. SUBURBAN HOME - NIGHT

I sit
alone

silent

tryi
ng
2
hold
back
tearz

a tele{vision} set
blasts

d
o
w
n
s
t
a
i
r
s

a journal.
a bed.
a pen.

I write:

Love is as cold as the ice storms in winter.

INT. MIND - DAY/NIGHT

T
O

NIGHT   *I*

are
we living
are we dying
are we here
are we there

FIND   *MYSELF*

[If the clock were forever would you be near?]

LOST   *IN*

THE   *ABYSS*

        is she thinking of me
        is she thinking of him
           have I lost her
           has she lost me

OF   *THOUGHTS*

            ?
            ?
            ?

INT. COMPUTER ROOM - NIGHT

Sink into this 70N3SOM3 chair

Internet connection……………………………………......
………………………………………………….on

Today, scientists discovered a black hole 13.0 billion light years away

the birth of the…

BIG BANG

```
        E   x   plo        sio         n
of                                     che
mic     a   l          st a r s
        pL   an E t s         m    a
t    t e      r                    m
ol   ecul              a      r
        s    t       r       u      c
tu         r   e
        h e a t           en     e r gy
wa t er
```

=

w (h) o ? (u) (man)

Has anything really changed ?

INT. BEDROOM - NIGHT

There's a glow in (HER)
    EyEz,
        She stares at me
    LOVE
      ?

        Dreamz
        mark
        the ability
        of man.

                She lays next
                    to me.

                I'm drunk.

      SHE:
    You sleeping?

    TOMMY:
      Yes.

Now, I'm thinking twice as much as I used to…

                      EOVL
                        SI
                      GULY
                    HEWN
                        TI
                    MNEAS
                OTHNIGN

Should've stayed in…

INT. CAR - NIGHT

Beach.
A clear **MOON** in the sky.
Alone.
4 got 10?

EYE 1'der...
...stretching
mind...

Note
(currently reading Zen and the Art of Motorcycle Maintainence)

I sit.
Looking out the window
at an empty dock.

A cool breeze...
I ask myself..

TOMMY: (V.O)
Should I go fill the void?

I exit car.

INT. KITCHEN - NIGHT

I sit at the table.
Head in arms.

MOTHER:
What's wrong?

I don't speak.

FATHER:
Are you lonely?

I look up.
Face red.
I can't speak.
Head back down.

TOMMY:
I don't know.

**out of the
desperation
of our hearts
all men fear
cowardice.

Is it wrong
not to admit
when a man's
been broken
down?

INT. JOURNAL - TWILIGHT

She is a budding rose. Her growth has left me empty, lost, forgotten.

I force myself to move on. That's all I can do. I know it's all I have.

My friends keep me occupied. My thoughts sometimes wander to her.

She kisses another man. Journal entries are prescribed for medication.

Sometimes I don't sleep. Time is linear only if you let go of the past…

INT. MIRROR - NIGHT

::sigh::

reflect
upon
body
----
trust
----
tsurt ←

TOMMY: (V.O.)
I know nothing of this shell
that keeps me chained.

…the door opens.
…I turn away from
this vehicle

…easing the mind…

EXT. BOAT – EVENING

full
moon

they
escape into the blackness
of the

Great South Bay

waves like glass

no sounds but the calming

br(ease)

SWOOOOOOOOOOSHHHHHHH!

Guas and I sit up front

while…

1 EYE'd WILL
drags on cigarette

ashes billowing the empty earth

the smoke too
escapes

…there's peace on this earth…

one
just has to
search
for it

EXT. DOCK - DAY

September…

Erosion of sand lines
correlate with the erosion of
heart beats.

BA BOOM
BA BOOM
BA BOOM

Fading.

A man rides his bicycle up on the dock
as I glance across at the million
dollar mansions stretched across the beach.
I hear him speak.

MAN:
(on cell phone)
Nothing is ever gonna get the best of me,
ya hear?

::I think to myself::

…except love.

INT. LOFT - DUSK

Unravel the leaf
(mr. dutchman)
trees stem from seeds
mind grows
till
mind knows

****

The universe expands
hubble bubble

(*   *   *)

pick your
po [.] int

Solar Bear

'cause this will
mark the beginning
of your journey.

www.ingramcontent.com/pod-product-compliance
Lightning Source LLC
LaVergne TN
LVHW021626080426
835510LV00019B/2779